A JOURNEY OF HOPE

Mercy Tobin

Mercy Tobin

LUCIDBOOKS

A Journey of Hope

Copyrighted © 2015 by Mercy Tobin
Illustrations by Mercy Tobin

Published by Lucid Books in Houston, TX.
www.LucidBooks.net

"Scripture quotations taken from the New American Standard Bible®, Copyright © 1960, 1962, 1963, 1968, 1971, 1972, 1973, 1975, 1977, 1995 by The Lockman Foundation Used by permission." (www.Lockman.org)

All rights reserved. No part of this publication may be reproduced, stored in a retrieval system, or transmitted in any form by any means, electronic, mechanical, photocopy, recording, or otherwise, without the prior permission of the publisher, except as provided for by USA copyright law.

First Printing 2015

ISBN-13: 978-1-63296-026-9
ISBN-10: 1632960265

Special Sales: Most Lucid Books titles are available in special quantity discounts. Custom imprinting or excerpting can also be done to fit special needs. Contact Lucid Books at info@lucidbooks.net.

TABLE OF CONTENTS

AN INTRODUCTION FROM A FRIEND ix

THE BEGINNING..1
   1.   ABOUT US..2
   2.   OUR STORY...6
   3.   OUR WRITING..8
   4.   THIS BOOK OF POEMS...9
   5.   THANKFUL...11
   6.   THE BIG MAN 12
   7.   SHARING OUR POEMS......................................13
   8.   WE HAVE A REASON 14
   9.   FOR THE READER..18

THE JOURNEY 19
   10. PAIN 20
   11. HOPE...21
   12. BLACK 22
   13. ENDLESS? 23

14.	SCREAMING	24
15.	BREAKING	25
16.	NO ONE	26
17.	BROKEN	27
18.	A NEW TIME	28
19.	ALONE	30
20.	SECRETS	31
21.	TOUCHING	32
22.	LIES	33
23.	THE BIG MAN, OUR HEALER	33
24.	THE OLD WAY	34
25.	THE NEW WAY	34
26.	LEARNING	35
27.	WORDS	36
28.	BRAVER	37
29.	WATCHING	38
30.	LISTENING	39
31.	HIS HOPE	40
32.	HE COMES	41
33.	JOY	42
34.	RAGS	43
35.	HOME	44
36.	DREAMS OF A LITTLE GIRL	45
37.	TRADING	46
38.	BRAVE FIGHTERS	47
39.	WRITING	48
40.	CHILDREN	49

41.	MALIE	50
42.	MORE ABOUT MALIE	51
43.	PEOPLE	52
44.	TIRED. AND STUCK	53
45.	SCARED	54
46.	HIS ANSWER	55
47.	RESTING	56
48.	LITTLE	57
49.	SEEING. AND WAITING	58
50.	MORE SECRETS	59
51.	DANCING WITH JOY	60
52.	TRUE NEEDS	61
53.	BAD	62
54.	PRETEND	63
55.	A NEW WAY	64
56.	HOLDING HANDS	65
57.	MYSTERY	66
58.	OUR BOY. OR MAN	67
59.	STILL THINKING	68
60.	STILL MORE THINKING	69
61.	FROZEN	70
62.	TIME	71
63.	SAFE	72
64.	OUR TEACHER	73
65.	HE IS WAITING	74
66.	WHISPERING HOPE	75
67.	WANTING	76

68.	TO SOME SCARED ONES	77
69.	LEFT OUT	78
70.	WORDS FOR A WORDLESS ONE	79
71.	MORE WORDS	80
72.	STILL MORE WORDS	81
73.	WATCHING HIM	82
74.	HELPING	83
75.	CHANGE	84
76.	A PROMISE	85
77.	OUR CRIES	86
78.	TELLING	87
79.	AN ANSWER	88
80.	LEARNING TO BE	89
81.	STAYING INSIDE	90
82.	NICE	91
83.	SAD	92
84.	CAN'T BE	93
85.	PRETENDING	94
86.	CONFUSED	95
87.	WATCHING. AND CONFUSED	96
88.	IS IT TRUE?	97
89.	HOW CAN IT BE?	98
90.	REAL!	99
91.	FLOWERS	100
92.	BEING HEARD	101
93.	MIXED UP	102
94.	DROWNING	103

95.	TERROR	104
96.	PLEASE HEAL	105
97.	HEROES OF A SPECIAL KIND	106
98.	ONLY YOU	107
99.	PRINCESS, OUR PUPPY	108
100.	HE KNOWS	109
101.	TRUTH	110
102.	OUR WORDS	111
103.	OUR SILENT CRIES	112
104.	HIS CHILD	113
105.	IN TIME	114
106.	FREEDOM	115
107.	ONE STEP	116
108.	HE DID IT	117
109.	A GIFT	118
110.	BEAUTY. IN UNEXPECTED PLACES	119
INDEX		121

AN INTRODUCTION FROM A FRIEND

My adventure with Mercy began in November 2007. Up until that time I had known Mercy as a quiet acquaintance in my circle of ordinary laundry-folding, grocery-shopping and kid-chauffeuring moms. I had delightedly accepted her invitation to share hot tea and a chat on her lovely deck overlooking a wooded creek in her back yard. As we cozied up in matching fleece blankets warding off the chill of the fall air, Mercy welcomed me over the threshold of her carefully constructed "normal" outer life into her complex and astounding hidden inner world.

Mercy's life tells the story of pure good versus pure evil. Her poems cover this spectrum as she expresses the darkness of the old time contrasted with the growing hope of a new time and a new way. As one might expect, the Hero of the story is Jesus – "the Real Jesus" as Mercy would say, or even better, her favorite name for Him: "the Big Man." This Big Man has been her Rescuer as long as she can remember and before she ever learned any other names for Him.

Some of Mercy's closest friends, dubbed "The Fellowship"

by a Tolkien fan (or two) in our midst, describe Mercy as "a flower unfolding in His beautiful hands." Mercy inspires us with her perseverance, her courage and her diligent hard work. She approaches life with simple yet profound faith, hopeful in her knowledge of this truth: the Big Man is real and He can and does talk to His children. She generously offers faithful love to her family, friends and neighbors, laying herself down for others with a pure heart of tender mercy and forgiveness. Mercy's poems describe her unique understanding of hope, courage, faith and love.

Mercy often thanks me for my friendship to her. I thank her for the blessed privilege of her gifts of trust and friendship to me.

Alleluia!

Barbara Boyd
November 2014

>The enemy has come to an end in perpetual ruins,
>And You have uprooted the cities*;
>The very memory of them has perished.
>But the Lord abides forever;
>
>The Lord also will be a stronghold for the oppressed,
>A stronghold in times of trouble;
>And those who know Your name will put their trust in You,
>For You, O Lord, have not forsaken those who seek You.

*guarded places
Psalm 9:6-7a, 9-10 (NAS)

The Beginning

ABOUT US

We
   have one body.
         But there are lots of us. Inside that body.

Ones, we call us.

Lots of ones, for lots of pain
that needed to be carried.
Too much
for only one person.

It is our Healer's gift,
               to us.
         He has made us, each one
for a time
when too much pain
would crush only one.

We are learning,
         that He has made us,
              with a purpose,
                   in His image.

       He,
           is three
               in One.

There are many more of us than three
and we have had walls,
and still usually do, between each. For protection.
We each have not known each other's pain
so we could still walk through life,
and not be crushed
from the weight
of what has been done
to us.

Now, we have been rescued,
           and are learning what it means
                      to be safe.

Slowly, our Healer is helping us see
        that we can be friends,
                and learn from each other
                        and from Him.

Each of us, is either, what we call
      an inside one
           or an outside one.

Outside ones are the ones
              brave enough
                      to be "out" by people.
          They have known less pain
than the inside ones.

Inside ones
hide inside,
for they carry
more pain
and are more scared
of people.

The deeper inside one comes from,
the deeper the pain
that one holds.

In the old time, we,
especially the inside ones, were taught,
that we each
were bad.

In this new time,
   our Rescuer and Healer,
      has given us each,
         His heart,
   and is teaching us
 that we were lied to.

In the old time,
we each,
both inside and outside ones,
had pain
that filled us.

In this new time,
    our Healer
      is setting us free
  from the ugly lies
and overwhelming pain.

Our story
        is a story of hope.

We,
        who once believed
we were the most bad
of the most bad,

              have been rescued by Him,

              who IS Hope.

And we
        have been given a place
                      with Him

              FOREVER.

OUR STORY

This is a story.
        A story of a journey.
                To be free.

We have a Maker of our journey.
            It is He who has rescued us.
And day by day,
    has been teaching us
        and loving us
           and setting us free.
Step by step. Day by day.

We wrote
    so inside ones
        could be heard.
But the writing
    has touched us all
      in ways we could
           never
              have imagined.
We wrote
    as we think.
Simply. With few words.
    But the feelings
        go deep.

We wrote
not for others.   But for us.

From writing and hearing
      each others' poems,
    we have become friends.

We have become thankful
       for the place each one has had
            and still is having
   in our story.

We hope that by reading our story
      "normal" people will see
that having "ones" inside
      is not terrible or bad or strange.

But instead
     a gift
         from the One who made us,
            as a way to deal with pain
        too big
    for only one
to hold.

We also hope
      that those who also have ones inside
         will see that they too
            have a Safe Place.
And that He is waiting to walk with them
               through their journey.

We hope most of all,
   that each who reads these poems, will see,
     a little clearer,
     our Rescuer,
        our Healer,
           our Hope.

And His amazing tender care for each of us
    in just the way
        each of us needs it.

OUR WRITING

Many inside,
maybe most,
cannot
or do not
speak.

It is especially them
    who need to be heard.

The Big Man, our Healer
    helps us know their thoughts and feelings
        then gives us words to match.

We, writers of these poems,
come from inside.
We used to think
that was bad.

Now, we are seeing
    that us being from the inside
        helps other inside ones
            know we understand,
        so are willing to share
    who they are
so that we can write it down.

First, they are heard by us,
    then as they get braver,
        they let the outside ones read about them,
            then safe people that we know,
then, sometimes, be put in this book.

THIS BOOK OF POEMS

This book
      is filled with poems
           written in the middle
                  of our journey.

The first years in this new time,
        was only in the beginning
                of our rescue.
Still so bound by scary lies
        all but a few
were afraid to write. And tell.

It was only now, in this middle time, in July 2014,
      our sister/friend and neighbor,
            lent us a children's book to read.
A story about a little girl, with troubles,
                who writes poems.

Our Healer used that story
        to help some inside
           want to try the same thing.

For the first time, we now have a way,
        for each one inside, to be heard,
      and let be known
all the fears, memories, and new joys
           as we each find ourselves held by a Healer
      who is loving us
and setting us free to tell our story, bit by bit,
      as each is ready.

Usually, in this book,

  each poem comes
     from a different one or group of ones,
    than the poem before.

The reader might begin to see
   ways we are and think and feel
the same as each other,
   and ways that we each are very different.

We have much to tell,
   and this book is only the beginning
        of our telling.

THANKFUL

Our poems
    come from our Healer.
Sometimes He simply gives them
    and we write them down.
Sometimes He gives us words
    to match what is in our hearts.
But all of it is possible
    because of what He has done
        and is still doing.
Directly, between Him and us.
    But also through special people.
        Those He has asked to walk alongside us
            on our journey.
The Fellowship.
    Special friends who have given in ways
        we didn't know possible
    and have loved us with His amazing love
        into this new way.
Our children.
    From the day they were born,
        they gave us a reason to be,
            a reason to keep going.
    And they still do.
There are no words good enough.

Other friends and even some people we don't know,
    that maybe without them knowing it,
        have been a way for us to see Him a little clearer.

Our Healer has touched us
        through each of these people,
           to help us learn this new way
        on our journey of knowing Him
           and becoming free.

THE BIG MAN

We are thankful
    that He
        who is called
            Jesus
        has many names.
    So that we
who have been
in scary places
where that name was used
to hurt us
and terrify us
        have other names we can call Him.
        While we heal.

Most of the names
    are in His book.

But the most special one to us
    comes from Him
        and what He did for us
            long ago
    in a very scary place
        when our body
            was very little.

Of all His names,
    He especially is
        and always will be
            the Big Man
                to us.

SHARING OUR POEMS

A friend touched us deep
          and helped us be braver
                  to share our poems.

We hardly know this friend,
      but she is sweet and gentle.
          She knows a little
                of our story.

When she heard
      we were making a book of our poems,
          she had tears
              and barely had words to tell
    the "yes!" that filled her up.

Our Healer
      is helping us see
          that our poems
              are not only telling
                  OUR pain and hope

but they are speaking
        for many people
            outside of us.

Maybe
    our Healer
        will use our poems
               to help other people,
      not just us,
         to have a way

          to be heard.

WE HAVE A REASON

Something
       in us
             is beginning
                    to change.
He,
   our Healer,
        is doing it.

So many times,
our body
has shaken
in fear.
Memories come.
Of being hated.
Hurt.
Not wanted.
People wanting us
to not be.
They tried.

      Our Rescuer
              stopped them.
                            Over and over.

Sometimes, they thought they were winning.
Our body seemed done.
We saw it, as our Rescuer held us over it.
      Then took us
           to the most amazing place of all.

Our Forever Home.

But He brought us back, to this home,
                            for a while, He said.
Because He had things yet, here, in this home,
                            that He had for us to do.

We are finally, beginning, to understand.
Many, many years have passed
                    since those times
                            in our Forever Home.

For a long time, those memories
seemed not real.

Not real, in the middle of years and years of pain
and being taught
how very worthless
we are.

But He, our Rescuer and Healer, remembered.
                              And knew they were real.

He is bigger
        than the biggest hurt
                than the biggest lies
                        even bigger than evil itself.

So, many years later,
                He has said,
                      it is time.

Time to make us free
></br>and bring hope
></br>and healing
></br>and help us know
></br>that we ARE real
></br>that our memories are real,
></br>and that HE wants us alive
></br>and to know healing
></br>and peace
></br>and joy
></br>and especially
></br>to know Him.

And that He
></br>had a reason
></br>for keeping us here
></br>instead of
></br>bringing us Home.

This morning, for the first time
></br>we began shaking
></br>with joy.
We
></br>are beginning
></br>to understand
></br>His reason.

As His little children
></br>held in His arms,
></br>we
></br>have a story to tell.

A story about
> our Rescuer
>> and Healer.

A story about
> who He is
>> and what He has done
> and is still doing
>> for us.

But not only for us.

> But for anyone who will hear
>> and listen

> and let Him take them too

>> in His arms

>> as His

>>> little child.

FOR THE READER

We wrote these poems
    as a journal.

Our way of telling
    our thoughts and feelings
        as we travel
            on our journey
                of healing.
And a way to remember
    how our Healer touches us each
        on that journey.

Except for the poems
    in this section, The Beginning,
each poem in this book
    is in the order it was written.

The reader can choose
    to read these poems
        in any order.

But they will make the most sense
    read in the order
        they were written.

The Journey

PAIN

Deep.
Covering everything.
Who holds it?
One?
No.
Maybe beginning with one.
But rising,
      building,
           overflowing
                 filling
                      and covering
                            each one.

The same way as hope
                 and peace
                       are now quietly,
            slowly,
         seeping in
    to bring

Change.

HOPE

Where did it come from?

Where did it start?

Who made it?

For so long
there was only
pain,
hurting,
and numbness.

What is this thing
        called hope?

Not one knows.

    Yet
        one by one
              each
                      is awakened
                              by it.

BLACK

The world is black.
The world is dark.
There is only hopeless,
unending night.

There is pain.
There is sadness.
Both too deep for words.

There is evil.
Terrifying, destroying
Evil.

The children cry.
There is black, dark,
Pain,
And evil.

ENDLESS?

The pain
touches
deep.

It makes room
for more pain.

How can it break
so much?

Will it
never
end?

Will it
always
fill us,
take over
and destroy
hope?

It's too big. This pain.
It has to be shared.
Many
have to help hold it.

Or there will be
no
tomorrow.

SCREAMING

There is
screaming
inside.
It is too big
to let out.
The pain of little ones
hurt
beyond words.

Will no one come?
Will no one help us?
Does no one see?
Does no one hear?

No one can come
because
no one
knows.
So the screaming
gets shut
further
and
further
in.

And the hope
becomes
hopeless.

BREAKING

The heart is breaking.
It has been shattered.
The pain is too big.
Too great for anyone
to hold.

Evil has come.
It comes to tear apart
and destroy.
Will it win?

The pain goes
on
and
on.
Evil comes.
It hates.
It works to destroy.
It knows nothing
of Hope.

The pain keeps going.
Evil keeps hating.
Evil thinks
it is winning.

More and more
evil comes.
It finds more and more
to tear apart
and destroy.

It is like
a burning fire.

NO ONE

The pain

burned

deep.

"We are

no one,"

they said.

"We can't

make it better,"

they said.

Hope

is

gone.

BROKEN

Broken.
Piece
by
piece.
Hated.
Each
one.

Broken
pieces
ready
to be
destroyed.
Gathered
into
a trash
pile.
Only
good
for
a trash
can.
Or fire.

Prepared
to be
completely
and
utterly
destroyed.

A NEW TIME

The hope
        comes in quietly.
One by one,
        it touches each one.

The hope feels strange.
        It doesn't seem real.

Some turn away from it.
        It can't be real, they say.

Some fight it.
        It's a trick, they say.
Some watch quietly
        as hope touches others.
How could something that good
        be for me, they say.

But hope keeps coming.
        Quietly, slowly,
                but it keeps coming.

Never pushing.
        Never forcing.

Just gently
        and tenderly

                He comes.

And one by one
        as each is ready
                He talks
with each one
            then gently lifts
that one
        onto

              His lap.

Hope has come.

He is bigger than any fear.

He is bigger than any evil.

He is quietly and gently
        pushing the fears away
                and filling us each

                with hope.

ALONE

I'm tough, says this one.
I don't need anyone, says that one.

But the pain is so deep, it feels like
a sharp knife
going through all of us.
And no words are left.

But the cries are there.
The hopeless, alone, cries.
        And we all cry with them.
But they don't know.
        They are so close,
yet so far away.

How to help them? We ask.
        And He gently lifts them   onto His lap.
You have friends, He says,
        as He holds them close.

But their pain is so deep,
        they can't hear us
Or even feel Him
        tenderly holding them.

Write, He says.
        Tell their story.
So we do. We help them be heard.
        And as we do,
             they quietly let us
                  take their hands
      As we all feel
             His peace
                      fill us.

SECRETS

Quiet.
Don't tell.
It's our secret.

In the dark corners,
each is hiding
with their secret.
Not knowing
that what they've been told
is not a secret,
but a lie.

But terrified
and alone
each
protects
their secret.

At a great price.

TOUCHING

We touched with someone today.
We don't mean the kind of outside touching.
We mean the way inside
      deep down
         touching.
We let her in.
      We shared us
           with her.
    Our pain,
        our sad,
           our hope.
And she let us
  inside her.

We like it. This new way.

People don't hurt us.
      They hurt WITH us.
People don't be angry with us.
      They are angry
         that others
      have hurt US.
They don't take away hope.
      They share their hope
         with us
           and help us
              believe the Big Man.

Then we are able to understand
      how touching
         in a thing called a hug
Is a telling
      of the inside touching
         that has happened.

LIES

Lies.
Ugly.
Hating.
Building walls.
Destroying.
Separating.

THE BIG MAN, OUR HEALER

He Is.
Beautiful.
Healing.
Breaking down walls.
Bringing Life.
Helping us to be friends.

THE OLD WAY

Scared.
Terrified.
Hiding.
Dying.
Separated.

THE NEW WAY

Peace.
Hope.
Free.
Alive.
Friends.

LEARNING

Scared.
Hoping.
Scared.
Not real.
Real?
How can that be?
But we're not real.
We are?
But what if…
There are no what if's?
How can that be?
Are YOU real?

No words.
No words
      for how big
           this new Safe is.
He is bigger
      and more real
           and more safe
               than we can even
           imagine.

He is too big for words.

           So we safely
               crawl into
                   His lap.

WORDS

Words.
      Beautiful words.

He helps us match them.
      Match them to tell
           each one's story.
So each one
      can be heard.

But sometimes…
      we run out.
So we wait…
      and listen
And He
      finishes
           with His words.

      And teaches us

                 Truth.

BRAVER

They help us be braver. These words.

Really it's He who gives us the words
        who helps us be braver.
But the words
        help us tell our story.
                So that each
                        can be heard.

As we are heard,
        we become braver.
Braver to be
        braver to feel
                braver to hope
                        braver to be alive
                              braver to be real.

And it helps us believe
        HIS words
                that started it all.

WATCHING

Scared.
Hiding.
Something….not sure what.
Too scared.
Wanting to run.
Wanting not to be.
Listening.
That "something" again.
No. Not for me.
Sad. Crying.
Quiet.
Watching.
That "something" again.
      But not knowing what.

But for us who are watching,
      and have been touched by it too,
We think quietly to ourselves,
      "It's called hope.
           That 'something'
               is called hope.
And soon it will fill you
      more and more,
          and you
              will be changed."
So we watch.
      and wait…
           for the One
              who IS Hope
To give that one
      more than she ever even imagined
           to be possible.

LISTENING

He
  is listening.
Now
  we are learning.

He has always
      been listening.
            And hearing.

Listening and hearing…
     our cries
         our pain
             our silence
                   that comes
            when the pain
       is too great.

He listens.

He hears.

And cries with us.

(Written for the ones inside who still cry without knowing)

HIS HOPE

"It's too hard.
         We can't even
                hope."

"That's okay,"
        He says.
              "I am holding hope
                          for you.
                                    You can rest."

So we let Him.

And we feel
        His peace
                cover us
                        and fill us.

HE COMES

Quietly He comes.
    Gently lifting each one
        from all the dark hidden places
          and carrying each
            to a new safe place.
"There are no rules," He says.
    "You don't have to stay here.
      I have made other safe places,
        there,
where you can hide
    but still
        be close,"
    He says, pointing.
    "But if you stay and listen,
        I will be your Teacher.
I have come to rescue you. Each one.
    I will teach you a new way.
I will heal the broken places
    and pain inside you.
I will protect you and help you.
    You will learn hope and joy and peace.
I have specially made each one of you
    and have a beautiful new name for each.
      You
        are my precious children."

So each decides to stay.
    Some choosing to be close to Him
and others hiding in the corners.
    But still listening and watching.
He sits down in the middle of us all
    and one by one
      teaches us about a way
        we have never known.

JOY

We watch
> as some little ones
>> who have once been
>>> so scared

Climb into His lap
> and snuggle
>> in His arms.

But their new joy
> is filling them
>> to overflowing.

So they stand up
> in His lap,
>> pat His face,
>>> and kiss
>>>> His cheek.

And He laughs
> with joy
>> along with them.

RAGS

Rags.
Dirty, torn rags.
    That's all
        that is covering
    each of us.
But one by one,
    He takes us
        to the Healing Stream
            in the Healing Meadow.
    And leads us
        into the cool, shallow water.
The sound of it is beautiful. *Psa 23*
    And we laugh
        as we watch tiny fish
            touch our toes
                in the clear, gently moving stream.
"I want to give you
        a new name
            and a new heart," He says,
    as He reaches down into the water.
He takes some water
        into His hands
            and He gently
                lets it run
                      over our head
                and sprinkles it
        over our shoulders.
The dirty rags
    are replaced
        with a soft, beautiful, white dress
            as the rags
    fall into the water and disappear

            Forever.

HOME

We laugh.
        We play.
                We twirl around
                        and dance.
The blue butterflies
            touch our noses
                    and tickle our hands.

We tumble on the grass with Him,
            giggling as we jump up
                    and play chase with Him
                            through the field of flowers.
We listen
        and join Him
                as He teaches us to sing Alleluia.
And the flowers and trees
        and EVERYTHING
                joins in,
                      each
                            in their own beautiful way.

The music flows in and around us,
                      different
                          than we have ever heard.
We have never known anything like it,
                but soon, He says,
                      soon, this will be
                            your forever Home.

And I will bring you back
                to stay.

DREAMS OF A LITTLE GIRL

Wishing.
Dreaming.
Stories built
      and details added.
Day
   after day
         after day.
Wishing.
   Dreaming.
      Yet knowing
  they would never
come true.

But the pain was so deep.
             The longing so strong.
Our stories gave us
            a place to be.
A home
    where we were loved.
               And safe.
So we created
     and planned
         and wished
            and dreamed.
And lived
     in our pretend world
because there was no place
for us
In the real one.

TRADING

I will make a trade, He says.

You give me your darkness
            And I will give you light.

Give me your pain.
              And I will give you joy.

I will give you hope
            for sadness.

Peace
     for terror.

I will take all that the enemy has done,
to hurt
and break
and destroy.
And I will show you
            that you are
                    My beautiful Child.

* Our Healer keeps telling this to each one inside

BRAVE FIGHTERS

We can't make it better.
Crying.
Sad.
Stuck.
Hopeless.
There's no way
   we can do it.
We can't be that way.
We've tried.
More crying.
More sad.
But then
      whispering,
            but really we don't want
      to be
that way.
But we're supposed to want it.
But really
   we hate it.
We hate that way.
And we hate being made
   to be that way.
Do we have to be
   that way?
      Can we really be free
         like the others
            that we've been watching?

    Could this new way
        really be for us too?

       Hoping.

      And watching.

WRITING

We
    have a story
           to tell.

Actually,
      many stories.
             Many
                  many
                      stories.
So we write,
      telling each one's story
              as they
                    are ready.

They thank us for writing,
        for helping them
                be heard.
But really
    it is them
        helping us.

In ways
    none of us

Understands.

CHILDREN

We were taught,
  and so believed
    that because we are children
We are
  stupid   too scared
    bad   too feeling
      hated   too little
and unable
  to take care of ourselves.

So we had to be punished.

Now we are learning
    that as HIS children
we are
  precious
    beautiful
      dearly loved
and knowing we need
      lots of help.
But NEVER
  getting punished.

But best of all,
  we are learning
    that as HIS little children,
      HE Himself is our Help.

And our favorite thing to do
    is to crawl up into His lap
      and feel His peace

  fill us.

MALIE

           She helped us be braver
      though she herself
was terrified.

Someone had hurt her,
and let her get sick
and matted
and dirty.

So she couldn't look at us
and crouched over
with her head
and her tail
down.

Each new thing
caused her
great fear.
And she wanted
to hide.

We understood.

We wanted
to hide
too.

MORE ABOUT MALIE

Terrified.
Dirty.
Sick.

We understood.
       And watched.
We knew what it was like
to have been hurt.
And to only want
to hide.

But we watched him,
    her boy,
          gently hold her
              and comfort her
                  and teach her
                      what safe is.

The same way
      that we now
            have Someone

        doing the same

         for us.

PEOPLE

People.
Scary.
Hurting.
Angry.
That's what we have known.
So we wanted to stay
hidden.
Forever.

But now…
        this new way
                and these new people…
They have kind eyes
        and kind voices
                and HOPE
                        that draws us out.
There's something inside us.
        For some
                something long forgotten,
        For others
                something never known.
But we feel it
        when we are with
                these safe people.
Then later
        we hold it
                and think about it
                      and wonder
                              what it is.

TIRED. AND STUCK

So tired.
So tired of being scared.
So tired of fighting this new way.
So tired of wanting to hide.

But……stuck.
Can't go back
Don't WANT to go back
to the old way.
But scared
      of this new way.
No….scared we won't fit
      in this new way.
Scared we will be
      the first ones to be told
We don't belong.

Big Man,
Is there a place for us too?

SCARED

We WANT to believe.
We really do.
But what if it's real,
And we can't belong?

What if all the safe,
       and all the kind,
              and all the good things
      we see others enjoying
isn't for us?

What if we're told no,
we can't come into the safe?
Where will we be?
What will we do?

We are so very
very
scared.

HIS ANSWER

He answers them.
    Those ones with such
big, scared questions.

He answers them.
It's not "what if?", my children, He says.

You already DO belong.
    You already HAVE a place.
        You already ARE my children.
You are loved.
    Greatly and deeply.
You are my precious
        beautiful
            children.
I will never leave you.
    Even when you can't feel it,
        I am holding you
            in My arms.
You are
    Chosen
        Beautiful
            Dearly Loved
And NO ONE
    can take your place.
I WANT you.
    And I want to give YOU
            all the safe
                all the kind
            and all the good things
        I've given to the others.
Welcome home, my children. Welcome home.
    And they ran into
        His arms.

RESTING

We have a place!
                they cried.
We belong to Him!
          We're His children!
                    His beautiful, precious children!
How can that be?
How can He want US?
How can He want to be by us?
He's so good, and we're so…

But He stops them.
I have given you my heart, He says.
        I am sharing my heart with you.
You have much to learn.
          And you will learn from my heart.
You will learn what precious children you each are.
        No longer hated,
                but dearly loved.

But come,
        rest now…
                and feel My peace.

So they snuggled further
                    into His arms.

LITTLE

We have been told lies
      about who we are.

Yes,
   we are little.
      Each one of us.
We thought
that was bad.
And terrible.
And hated.

Now, we are finding out
     that being little
           is
               a special gift.

We are little
     so He helps us.
We get scared
     so He comforts us.
We can't get it right
     so He teaches us
         and loves us
            and tells us
               we still have a place.

And so...
     as His little children....

          we
            climb up into His lap
              and rest.

SEEING. AND WAITING

Still they cry,
        "We have a place!"

But now
        these are tears
                of joy
                      and hope
                              and peace.

And it fills them
        to overflowing.

And touches
        each one
                of us.

And together,
        we long for the time,
                when each one
                          will know
                                this truth.

MORE SECRETS

We were supposed to make it better.
(Secrets)
But we WERE.
We don't even know how to try any more.
We just keep hurting and hurting.
The hurt is too big.
We don't know what to do with it.
So we get scared.
So very very scared.
So we want to run and hide.
Or cry.
But we can't do either.
Because we're supposed to fix it.
(Secrets)
We're supposed to be good.
And do it right.
And a whole bunch more stuff.
(More secrets)

But now
    we want to tell.
        Because we've been watching.
            We like this new way.
    Or think we do.
But we're scared.
So very very scared.

How can we be okay if we have
        so many secrets?

DANCING WITH JOY

There's dancing inside tonight.
                                        Lots.

Ones who thought
they were trapped
with so many secrets

        Found out
                they are free.

The ones who only
wanted to hide

        are now
                dancing
                        with joy.

For He
    has taken their secrets…
            and given them joy
                and peace
                    and laughter.

They made a trade with Him.
        They have given Him
their secrets…
        And He
            has made them
                    free.

And He picks them up
        and dances
              with them

As He
    and they
        cry
            with joy.

TRUE NEEDS

We worried
      about a friend today.

She called
      to talk.

But we
      couldn't.

He,
   the Big Man,
         told us,

That's okay, child.

She needed you…

But she needed
         Me

            more.

BAD

We're scared.
We don't like being us.
We're bad.
We're supposed to be bad.
We're not supposed to ever try
       to be good.
Or even want to. (We were told.)
Or else really bad,
scary things
will happen.
But we don't want to be bad.
      We've started peeking. And watching.
          We're not by scary people
              any more.
And others inside
who were bad
       are learning
            they're not.
We've watched them
     come out
        and be with
           these new, nice people.
          The ones
              with the kind eyes.
And it makes us
     want to lose
         OUR bad
            too.
But we don't know how.
But we want to lose it
        so very much.
We hope
     we will find
          a way.

PRETEND

Our pretend
       has started falling off.
              Like a mask.
                     Or a costume.
            Or something so big and heavy,
      that with it covering us
we could hardly breathe.
Or be.
But now
       it has begun to fall off.
One by one,
       we are each beginning
             to let go of the lies we've been told…
About who we are supposed to be…
Or not be.

But as our pretend falls off,
     we wonder…
               Who are we really?
               Are we really real?
               Is it safe to be real?
               Is it safe to WANT
                     to be alive and real
      and have feelings and thinkings like real people?
Will we really not be by scary people ever again?
What if we let go of all the lies? And all the pretend?
Who will we be? What will we be like?

But something we just realized…
It's not just the outside that's changing,
      but we each are changing way deep inside.
And the pretend falling off
      is happening
           because of all that change.

A NEW WAY

We have begun
        to tell our story.

How we are
           feeling
                 and thinking
                         and being.

It touches us each
        as we begin to understand
                each other's pain,
                      and fears
                            and hopes.

And as we watch Him
            who IS Hope
                tenderly care
                      for each one.

And whisper to them
            gentle words
                    of truth.

HOLDING HANDS

We like this new way…
        Of being friends with each other
Of being kind and gentle,
        and helping one another,
Of sharing our pain…
              and hope…
    and crying
        with the ones who cry.

"He has come! He has come to help us!
        You don't need to hide any more,"
            we tell the ones
                still scared and hiding.
"He has come to heal our pain,
                    and make us free!"

And we cry with joy
        as one by one,
             they are touched
                    by Him
                        and then come

And hold hands
        with us.

MYSTERY

This telling
        and sharing
                our stories…

It's doing something
      inside.

It is bringing
        hope
            and peace
                and joy.

But more…
      But we don't have words.

But wait!
      We know!

It's that…
      we are becoming
               friends…

And touching each other
                in ways
                    we didn't know
                        possible.

OUR BOY. OR MAN

We met a man tonight.
Well really, the outside ones say,
      we met a boy. Our boy.
But he seems like
          a man to us.
                A really nice man.

He has kind eyes
      and a kind voice too.
            Just like those nice ladies
            we have met.

We were watching
      while he talked with outside ones
                who know him.
Then one of us inside ones came out.
            But lots of us
                were close by
                    watching.

We didn't think we would ever do
                    something like that.
Because men are scary.
            But not this one.

Maybe there are other nice ones too.
We will watch
          and see.

STILL THINKING

Others are thinking
                about that boy-man too.
We can hear them.
They were watching too.
We will think with them.

We are all wondering.
Why was he so nice
                to the one who came out?
He didn't be angry
                at all.
He didn't say
                mean, scary things.
He even acted
                like he liked that one!
He didn't want us
                to be "big"
                        or "one".
He just kept being kind.

We have to think about this some more.
Hmmm… maybe…
    maybe
          he's being matched
                    with the Big Man.
He sure reminded us
              of Him.

Still thinking.

STILL MORE THINKING

Still more ones are joining us.
      Thinking about that boy-man, we mean.
They're thinking,
      "That boy-man is real. And nice.
And we can see him
      with our eyes.
We can see the Big Man
      on the inside
           with our eyes,
      but not on the outside.
We were taught,
      that everything on the inside
           is not real.
Especially us.
But that boy-man is real.
And he matches the Big Man.
Maybe the Big Man is real too.
And all that He has been telling us.
Maybe He really DID rescue us,
      and maybe we really ARE safe now.
And maybe we really are real.
Maybe. Maybe so."

Still thinking.

FROZEN

Bigger than words scared.
Too scared to feel, scared.
Too scared to be.
Frozen.
Without hope.
Afraid to be.
Afraid to feel.
Afraid to hope.

What has been done to you, little ones?
That the fear is so big
         that it takes away your words,
And makes you terrified to be?

Yet there are many like this.
         So very, very many.
How will they hope, and feel, and laugh?
How will they heal?
Their pain is too big for them to hold.

We wait… and watch.

Then silently
            and gently
                        He comes.
He comes
      to hold their pain
                  and give them a place

         To be.

TIME

He comes.

We watch
      as He comes.

He picks them up.
          Gently, tenderly.
He knows their pain.
He knows every detail.
He knows what took away their words.
He knows what took away their hope.

He will help them.
      He will hold them.

But they need time.
         Time to rest
                in His arms.

SAFE

I've gained a friend today.
        Not right away though.
Making a friend takes time.

I've felt her watching for awhile.
        How long, I don't know.
But today I could feel her strongly.
        Her pain, her hopelessness, her terror.
            But mostly her terror.
And so, she was terrified to move or be.
        Or even make a sound.
Frozen.
        But watching.
I could feel the "not real"
        that she so wanted to be.
So much that I began to wonder
        if I was real.

But HE was watching.
        He who REAL comes from.
I saw Him and I remembered who I am.
        I asked Him for help
            and loved His ideas!
As I played peek-a-boo
        with this little one,
He helped me know how
        and when
            to add a word or two
                of truth with the peek-a-boos.
As she giggled while we played,
        the words began snuggling down inside her,
            and she soon quietly took my hand,
                then snuggled with me
                      and peacefully fell asleep.

OUR TEACHER

It's amazing
    how He knows
        how to help
            each one.

Each one
    has different needs
        and fears

And their own story.

Only He knows
    what each one
        needs to hear
            or see
                or experience
To begin believing this new way.

And He does it.
    One by one.
        As each is ready.

He gently,
    tenderly
        helps each
            understand the truth

Of who we are
    and how He has come
        to set us

        FREE.

HE IS WAITING

What is it, little one?
        What is causing your fear that we feel?
What has been done to you
        that you are terrified to sleep?
How we long to help comfort you
      and help you know
           the One who IS Comfort.

Please, won't you take our hands?
        We want to be your friends.
We want you to know
      that the things you fear
          will no longer happen.
For we have a Rescuer.
        He has brought us to a safe place.
           He will calm our fears.
               and heal our pain.

That terror you feel -
      He will take it
          and give you peace instead.

He will help you know His Safe,
        And make you want to laugh
               and dance
                   and sing.

He has all this waiting for you
              and more.

For you
      are His beloved
             child.

WHISPERING HOPE

We want to whisper hope to you.
        You who are so terrified of the night.

We long for you to know His safe
        and the tears He cries for you.

You are His precious child,
        His beloved,
               His beautiful one.

        He has a place for you.

Not one of hurting.
Or pain.
Or hate.
        He wants you to be free.

        He wants you to know,
deep down inside you,
that there is no blame
or hate
or punishment.

        He has come to make you free.
        He has come to show you Truth.

You have been lied to
and tricked
and hurt.

But our Rescuer says,

        "No more!"

WANTING

Little ones,

You have been terrified to speak.
    So we have whispered hope.

You have been terrified to hope.
    So we have hoped for you.

You have been terrified to be.
    So we have come to hold your hand.

But now we have come to listen.
    For we long to know your story.

And we have come to share your tears
    For we long to share your pain.

We have come to hold your hand.
    For we want you to be.

TO SOME SCARED ONES

It's hope that we feel -
        that new feeling from you.
So small, it's barely there.
        But it's there, we're sure.

And we can tell our tears
        have been joined by yours,
As hope reaches down
            and touches you.

We touch your hand,
        and you don't pull back
in fear.

It's something so little,
           but it's enough.
Enough
    to help us remember
               that HE
                      is keeping you safe,
And holding us each.

And helping us become friends

                as we touch each other

                          with hope.

LEFT OUT

A friend is sad today.
A deep kind of sad.
And we are sad with her.
And ask Him
      who is Comfort
             to hold her.
                    And help her.

Her sad is big.
Because it's about being left out.
It goes deep within her.
And us.
Because we thought we were alone
      with that kind of sad.
And that we have it because
      there is something wrong with us.
But this friend - she's not that.
    She's dearly loved.
           And a treasure.
                    And wanted.

And yet she feels left out too.

Maybe it's not just us. Maybe we're not bad.
Maybe there's something bigger
    and deeper
        than we understand.

So we have asked Him

            to teach us.

WORDS FOR A WORDLESS ONE

Scared.
Too scared.
Have to run away.
But can't.
Too scared.
Want to hide.
But can't. Not all the way at least.
Because the scared is too big.

But it's not just that.

What is this thing that pulls me out?
I don't want it.
                But I do.
I want to run away.
                But I don't really.
Why not?
What is this thing?
And why do I feel it from the others?
What made them feel it?
Why do I want it so bad I want to cry?
But I don't trust it. Or believe it's real.
How can I?

But I like it. I think.
     So I let it pull me out.
                      Further
                            and further.
But I'm too scared.
So I hide again.

MORE WORDS

Bad.
I'm too bad.
That's why I'm so
scared.

I want the others to know.   Me.

I want them to find out.   I'm here.
But I don't.

I'm too bad.
And too scared.

Why does something pull me out still?

I pretend I don't want it.   But I do.
But I don't know what it is.
        But I still want it.
                I still hope that I can have it.
But I don't know what it is.

        Why does it call me out?

                Why do I want it so much?

STILL MORE WORDS

      It's still pulling me.
That thing.
      It's still pulling me out.
It's hard work to be   pulled out.
      But I let it.
           Because I want it.
                  Somehow.
But I don't know why.

But I get scared.
So I pull back.
Again
and again
and again.

      But I want it so much.
But I don't know why.
      But I want it enough to let it pull me.

But I'm . . . . bad.
Why is that getting smaller?
What is eating it?
What can make bad go away?
I don't understand.

I don't have to, He tells me.
I can just rest, He tells me.
There will be time for understanding, He says.
But for now, just rest.

You've worked hard tonight. I'm proud of you.

Proud? Of me? Why?

           I wonder.

WATCHING HIM

We're proud too, of this one.
    For we've been watching too.   With Him.

We wonder what her story is.
    Why she thinks she's so bad.
But we know, really.
    In a way.
We've believed we were bad too.
        Until we were set free.
            By Him.

By Him, who holds us now.
    And helps us.
        And comforts us.
            And changes us inside.
                And helps us believe truth.
About Him. About us.
And about what's been done to us.

But that we are safe now. Very safe.
    Way more than we can understand.
        But more and more,
            we feel His safe
        filling us
        and surrounding us
In a way we have never known.

So we keep asking Him, the Safe One,
    to do the same
        for this so very scared one.

So that she will be pulled out too,
    by this very same,
        amazing Safe
           of His.

HELPING

Scared.
No, terrified.
    Yet still watching.

We think they're brave.
    They could just hide.
        But they don't.

They want to see this new safe.
    But there are people in this new safe.
They're terrified of people.
    But these are kind people, we explain.
People who will help us and Tobie
    learn more together how to help other people.
Because we make a good team, we're told.

We think so too.

We take care of Tobie.
    But in a bigger way,
        he takes care of us.
Each one.
    In the way each needs.
And what he's learned in helping us,
        we together can use
            to help other people.

We're scared too, we tell those inside ones.
    But together we can all watch.

And together learn about a new safe.
    And Tobie will be right by our side.

CHANGE

We have a friend
      who told one of us
           a simple thing
                one day.

But for us,
      it turned
           some things
      upside
down.

Change is safe, she said.
It's okay to try something,
      then change your mind,
           and try something different.

That went in deep.
      And the news spread.
But it took time to believe.
      And still we are learning.
           And trying that new way.

With arranging rocks,
      and trying new foods,
           and writing poems.
And with all that trying,
           we are learning,

To think
      and feel
           and be.

A PROMISE

Panic.
Woke up at 4 A.M.
Panic.

How can we tell those terrified ones
        THAT time
                is gone
                      forever?
Our Protector has promised
        that will never happen again.

How can we tell them and help them believe
        that we have been rescued?
That we have a Rescuer
        so amazing,
             and so mighty,
                  that He can do anything He wants.

And He WANTS to
            and WILL
                      keep us safe. Forever.
That old time is gone. Forever.

For He Himself has said, "Enough!" "No more!"

How can we help those ones believe?
                          And know the truth?
We can't
But He can.
We only need to wait.
                And watch.
                            And listen.
He WILL do it.
            He has promised.

OUR CRIES

We cry out.
        To Him, our Rescuer.

Please help these terrified ones.
Please help them know You are real
              and holding them even now.
Please help them know this safe is real
              and they will never be hurt like that again.

Our hearts cry out.
        And WITH these terrified ones.

Please help them know Your truth.
        And Your amazing love for each of us.
That we are precious to You and safe
        And that now we EACH have a place to be.

Please heal their pain.
        And ours.
Please help them know these aren't just words.
        But real, deep, and longing cries.
For them.
        From us.
              To You.

TELLING

People want to know what He looks like.
        What color of hair? How long?
                The color of His eyes.
But we don't see Him that way.
His color could be purple!

But it's still HIM!
                It's HIM.
Who never changes.
        Who never goes away.
                Who always keeps us safe.
He will always BE.
        And we with Him.
                Safe.
                      Precious.
                          Dearly loved.
        In the best place of all.

Maybe that's what they really want to know.
                      Those who ask, we mean.
And so we say,
        Yes, His eyes touch you deep,
                way inside.
His arms hold you close.

        And when He laughs,
                joy goes through you
                      like you have never known.
So yes. You can ask.
        And we will tell you.
Yes. He is real.
        And alive.
                And loves you more
                      than you can even imagine.

AN ANSWER

We've been waiting.
      Waiting to visit a friend.
           Who will soon go Home.

But He, our Wisdom, told us, "No, not now.
      Wait. And listen. I will tell you when."

So we waited. And listened.
      And waited and listened some more.
           Hoping it wouldn't be too late.

But with Him, there is never a "too late".
      For He has a perfect plan
          and He knows what He is doing.
Even when we don't.

So we waited some more. And almost forgot.
      To listen.

But when He spoke, we remembered.
      We remembered we were listening. And waiting.
And we remembered something else.

A question our friend had asked. On another visit.
      A question that has an answer
          that we knew with our heart,
                but didn't have words.

This morning, the One who IS our Answer,
                gave us the words.
Now we know why we've waited.

Our friend needs that answer
          before he leaves to go Home.

LEARNING TO BE

Learning to be
        is lots like

Learning
      to walk.

One
    step
        at
           a
              time.

      With
          others
              cheering
                    us
                        on.

STAYING INSIDE

We don't like being by people.
They're not nice to us.
They hurt us lots.
So we hide.

If we could do it right,
       we could be by them.
              Maybe.

But then they'd find out we're bad
       inside us.
So they would hate us.
And hurt us.

Then it would start over again.
The punishing, we mean.

Others inside might get hurt instead of us.
Then it would be our fault.
So we better stay
inside.

We don't like us.
We wish we weren't
so bad.

NICE

There are nice ones
inside.

Really nice ones.

We wish we could be
                like them.

But we can't.

We don't know how.

Sometimes we
cry.

We wish we
            could be nice too.

SAD

There are people by us sometimes.
        Really nice people.

We don't know why they're so nice.

    We wish we could find out.

Maybe then
        we could be good
                and they
                        would be nice
            to us
                    too.

But we don't know how
      to be good.

So we can't be by them.

So we get sad.

CAN'T BE

The Big Man
          tells us
                  we're good.

But really,
He must not
know
US.

We're
the
bad
ones.

That's why
we're hated.
And bad.
And have
to be
punished.

Because
we can't be
what
we're supposed
to be.

PRETENDING

We
pretend
we don't
have
feelings.

But
    we do.

So

we

hide

them.

Way

deep

down

inside

us.

So we

can be

safe.

CONFUSED

Why
    do people be nice to us,
Even
    when they know about us?

Why
    don't they
hate us,
and hurt us,
like
we were told
they would?

Why
    instead
        are they nice,
            and have kind eyes
                and gentle words?
Why
    do they tell us
        the Big Man
            loves us
instead
of hates us?

Why
    do they do
        everything opposite

Of what
we were told
they would do?

WATCHING. AND CONFUSED

There
        are some brave ones
inside.

They
        be by
              people.

We
        watch them.

We watch them
              not get punished.

We watch them
              not get hurt.

We watch them
              not be scared
                      of these people.

We cry.

But we don't

know why.

IS IT TRUE?

Big Man,
        please help us.

We're scared too.
        We've been watching too.

It almost seems
        that all You've been telling us

Is real
        and true.

How can that be?

We are still us.
        But we're not being punished.

No one is being punished.
        Not even ones who be by people.

What is this new way?

Are You really real?
        And true?

Is it true that we are safe?
        No matter what?

Did You really do all this?

For us?

HOW CAN IT BE?

How can there be
         a place
                 for us?

How can we
         not have
                 to go away?

Is there really
         a safe for us?

Are we really
         real?

Can we be by people
         and not be hurt?

How can that be?

How can everything we've known
         be changed
                 Forever?

REAL!

We
        are people.

We're finding out.

We
        are real.
                And alive.
                        And can think
                              And feel
                                    And hope
                                          And be.

How is it possible?
How did it happen?
How is it safe?
How do we get to be us?

Without punishing
Or rules
Or being rid of?

How do we get to stand up

                      and be?

FLOWERS

It's a time
        of learning.

And discovery.

        And hope.

And of learning
                to be.

It's like watching
    a flower bud
        slowly open.
Except
        that it's us.

We aren't just one flower.
    But many.

Many, many beautiful flowers,
                He has said.

And He has also said,

    "There are NEVER
            too many flowers!"

BEING HEARD

Writing.
    Writing and listening.

        And bringing hope.

We are learning
    that being heard
        helps hope come.

So we listen.
    And let them tell
        and share

Their pain.
Their cries.
Their memories.

And we
    in listening
        share with them

        our Hope.

MIXED UP

Terrified.
Crying inside.
Can't make it better.
Being too bad.
Don't want to tell
secrets.
Being bad.

Because of wanting to tell
secrets.

Terrified.
Frozen.
Don't want to move.
Or think.
Or feel.
But it keeps happening
      anyway.
Why?

Terrified to be real.

But desperately wanting to be.

DROWNING

It
feels

like
drowning.

So
covered
and filled
with pain.

And terror.

It
becomes
hard
to
breathe.

Gasping.

Terrified.

Desperately

terrified

to

be.

TERROR

No words.
No movement.
Just terror.
Terrified to move.
Terrified to speak.
Terrified to think.

The pain.
It fills and covers.
It tears at her very being.

How can someone be so cruel
To so hurt such a little one?

We who watch
can feel her pain.
And see her terror.

But the horror of her memories
Are too huge
for all of us.

Especially her.

PLEASE HEAL

Big Man, our Rescuer,
We see this precious one of yours.

Her pain is too big.
Her terror too great.
For us to help.
For her to let us.

We long to help
But it's like a huge mountain.

Please touch her.
        And help her.
                And bring her peace.

We cry for her.
And feel the cries within her.
That she can't let out.

Please touch her.
        And help her know Your safe.

Please help her
        laugh
                and play

        And be
            FREE.

HEROES OF A SPECIAL KIND

More and more
We outer ones
Are beginning to understand
The price
      that has been paid
To keep us safe.
We are beginning to know
      these
Wordless ones.
And their pain.
And terror.
And the memories
      that so fill them.

They have taken
      what was meant for us.
On themselves.

They are
      brave fighters.
Heroes
      of a special kind.

It is a privilege to know them
      and share their pain
           and give them a special place

As we all snuggle
          in our Rescuer's
                arms.

ONLY YOU

Our dear Big Man,

You have said that what we do,
      is not complaining.
           But pouring our hearts
                  out to You.

Big Man,
      We have very full hearts today.
Full of the pain and sadness and fears
      that we can feel from so many.

We cry for them.
      They are too terrified to cry.

We hurt with them.
      But their hurt is bigger than we know.

We hope for them.
      They have lost theirs.

But only You
      know every detail
          of their pain,
    their terror,
        their story,
            their heart.

      Only You

           can heal them.

PRINCESS, OUR PUPPY

Growing up,
      our parents wondered,
           why we liked our puppy
                  so much.
"It's not normal",
      they would tell us.
"only a short time with her a day is allowed."
And many other things about us
      that we don't want to remember.

But our puppy loved us.
      And didn't hurt us,
          or call us stupid or dumb
                or stuck-in-a-hole.

She didn't tell us how bad we were
      or all the things wrong with us.
She simply snuggled
         on our lap,
             happy to just be with us

      and give us
         a safe place
             to be.

HE KNOWS

The Big Man
      helped us today.
In a way
      we didn't know we needed.
To help a need
      we didn't understand.
To us,
      the problem looked simple.

But it was causing pain
deep inside.
And scared.
And sad.

But we didn't know why.
      But He did.
           Because He knows our hearts.
He knows the pain,
and scared,
and sad
of each one.

He knows every detail.

So He brought help.
      In a way
           we would never
                have guessed.
Because
      it had nothing to do
           with the problem.

The problem WE could see.

TRUTH

Oh, little ones
who are hurting so badly,

We long
      for you
            to know
                  the truth.
For you to know
            that now we are free.
Never to be punished again.

You
      have a place.   Yes, you.

You will never be made
to go away.
You will always be wanted.
                And loved.
                    And treasured.
He
   who is our Hope
            is also our Rescuer.
He has given us
            all these things
                    and more.
He has come to
        free us
            and heal us
And tenderly,
      gently
         hold us.
            Forever.

OUR WORDS

Words
        are funny things.

We thought
        learning big ones
                and using lots
Would make us sound big
        and grown-up.

But our Teacher
        has been teaching us
                that us being little
Is a special gift.

And that our little words
        are special too.

There are also
        many of us
who are very quiet.

Our Teacher
        is helping us
                use our little words
    that are not very many

To tell about us
        and to tell about Him

    Through our eyes.

        And our hearts.

OUR SILENT CRIES

Our cries
were silent.
But there.

Locked way inside
so no one
could hear a sound.

      Except Him.

Him. The One who made our bodies
    so that we COULD cry,
        when we needed to.

Him. Who could still hear us
    when we couldn't make a sound.
        So He came.

He came to rescue us.
    Even when we had no hope.
        Even when our cries were silent.

And now, one by one, He is letting each know
    That He has heard, and still hears,
Each one's
    silent cries.

And one by one
    He is giving each

A voice
    and a way
        to be heard.

HIS CHILD

Evil is real.
And alive.
And terrifying.
                But bigger than evil,
        even bigger than the biggest mountain
     compared to the tiniest ant,

        Is the biggest of big,
          the most real of real,
      and more alive than we knew possible,
One who is Mighty
           and Strong
                and more Good
                      than we can even imagine.
HE IS
      where real comes from,
          how "alive" was made,
                how everything came to be.

        He holds everything there ever was,
              and is,
         and is still yet to come
            in His hands.
    And yet,
        He holds us each,
           one at a time,
      in His arms,
         as if we are His only,
        dear,
        specially loved
        and treasured

            child.

IN TIME

We want so
        to protect
                these terrified ones.

We too, were once terrified
        We've each had our turn.
Memories we don't want to think about.
        Or remember.

But these ones are even more terrified.
        They barely seem real. Or alive.
They lost wanting to be
        long ago.

He, our Rescuer, will come and help them.
        We have seen it many times.
                And it has been done for us.

He alone knows what each needs.
            He alone can heal their pain
                      and bring them hope.

                And joy.

He alone knows when the time is right.

But until then,
        we will watch.
                And wait.

        And share our hope

                with them.

FREEDOM

We outside ones
    have had lots of ideas.

Ideas of what we can do
    with our new freedom.

And many of those things, we have tried.
                           And enjoyed.

Freedom changes everything.
        How you think. And feel. And laugh.

It makes you want to discover.
                 And learn.
                       And hope.
But it also helps you see better.
    And hear more clearly.
  And especially
      to see others who are hurting.
          And hear their cries.
                And want to share their pain.

So that they too
            can find this freedom.
Or rather
    that they
        can let themselves
           be found by Him.

Him. Who IS Freedom.

Where all true freedom
            comes from.

ONE STEP

We feel their cries now.
Those terrified, silent ones of the night.

Still no sound, but very real cries.
        We can all feel them
from deep inside.

Their silent cries
        touch each one of us.

With sadness, yes.
        And so we cry with them.

                But also with hope.

For a cry, even though silent,
      is one step
            towards this new time.

One step
      towards feeling
           and thinking
                and being.

Instead of being frozen

In fear.

HE DID IT

We have a friend
      who touched us deep tonight.
And helped those terrified ones
      of the night.
Just by being her.
          Safe.
                Listening.
                      Wanting to understand.
It helped them know
      this new way is real.
                      And true.
It helped them start believing - just a little -
      that maybe we really are
                      safe.
We think she had no idea
      the curiosity she was causing,
            and the hope she was bringing,
As she sent us a bedtime prayer
      that she was praying over us.

It brought tears of hope.
                      And peace. In them.
And thankfulness in us
      for how He once again
           has answered our prayers
      and allowed us to watch
           how He never fails
          to touch
                such hurting ones.

A GIFT

We have a privilege
                and a gift
                              that our Giver has given us.

We used to think the opposite,
        but now,
                He is helping us see the truth.

We are many
        and little,

Made and dearly loved by Him.
                Each one.

And He NEVER makes mistakes.

He has been showing us
                        how that is a gift.

But a very special thing,
        is that having so many
                gives us so very many times
                      to watch Him do
                              amazing things
in someone else,
        as we watch Him touch,
                one by one
                        each one inside.

BEAUTY. IN UNEXPECTED PLACES

Our Healer
    touches our lives
        in more ways
            than we can understand.
Sometimes, He does it simply
    and directly
        from Him.
Sometimes, He does it through people, animals,
    and ways we would never imagine.

He is constantly
    bringing hope
        where there is none,
            comfort where there are tears,
        and in the middle of a broken world,
    somehow, amazingly,
takes each broken thing
    and changes us,
        who are touched by it.

Then we begin to understand
            that HE
        is bigger than evil,
    than sickness,
  than death,
or than any other terrible thing.

And that amazingly,
    He takes even the worst there is
        and makes beauty
            shine from it.
And through it.
    And uses it
        to heal us.

INDEX

ABOUT US, 2
A GIFT, 118
ALONE, 30
AN ANSWER, 88
A NEW TIME, 28
A NEW WAY, 64
A PROMISE, 85

BAD, 62
BEAUTY. IN UNEXPECTED PLACES, 119
BEING HEARD, 101
BLACK, 22
BRAVE FIGHTERS, 47
BRAVER, 37
BREAKING, 25
BROKEN, 27

CAN'T BE, 93
CHANGE, 84
CHILDREN, 49

CONFUSED, 95

DANCING WITH JOY, 60
DREAMS OF A LITTLE GIRL, 45
DROWNING, 103

ENDLESS?, 23

FLOWERS, 100
FOR THE READER, 18
FREEDOM, 115
FROZEN, 70

HE COMES, 41
HE DID IT, 117
HE IS WAITING, 74
HE KNOWS, 109
HELPING, 83
HEROES OF A SPECIAL KIND, 106
HIS ANSWER, 55
HIS CHILD, 113

HIS HOPE, 40
HOLDING HANDS, 65
HOME, 44
HOPE, 21
HOW CAN IT BE?, 98

IN TIME, 114
IS IT TRUE?, 97

JOY, 42

LEARNING, 35
LEARNING TO BE, 89
LEFT OUT, 78
LIES, 33
LISTENING, 39
LITTLE, 57

MALIE, 50
MIXED UP, 102
MORE ABOUT MALIE, 51
MORE SECRETS, 59
MORE WORDS, 80
MYSTERY, 66

NICE, 91
NO ONE, 26

ONE STEP, 116
ONLY YOU, 107
OUR BOY. OR MAN, 67
OUR CRIES, 86
OUR SILENT CRIES, 112

OUR STORY, 6
OUR TEACHER, 73
OUR WORDS, 111
OUR WRITING, 8

PAIN, 20
PEOPLE, 52
PLEASE HEAL, 105
PRETEND, 63
PRETENDING, 94
PRINCESS, OUR PUPPY, 108

RAGS, 43
REAL!, 99
RESTING, 56

SAD, 92
SAFE, 72
SCARED, 54
SCREAMING, 24
SECRETS, 31
SEEING. AND WAITING, 58
SHARING OUR POEMS, 13
STAYING INSIDE, 90
STILL MORE THINKING, 69
STILL MORE WORDS, 81
STILL THINKING, 68

TELLING, 87
TERROR, 104
THANKFUL, 11
THE BIG MAN, 12

THE BIG MAN, OUR HEALER, 33
THE NEW WAY, 34
THE OLD WAY, 34
THIS BOOK OF POEMS, 9
TIME, 71
TIRED. AND STUCK, 53
TO SOME SCARED ONES, 77
TOUCHING, 32
TRADING, 46
TRUE NEEDS, 61
TRUTH, 110

WANTING, 76
WATCHING, 38
WATCHING. AND CONFUSED, 96
WATCHING HIM, 82
WE HAVE A REASON, 14
WHISPERING HOPE, 75
WORDS, 36
WORDS FOR A WORDLESS ONE, 79
WRITING, 48

CPSIA information can be obtained
at www.ICGtesting.com
Printed in the USA
LVHW041244200819
628220LV00005B/8/P